A COLLECTION OF
Jewish Brainteasers, Puzzles, and Enigmas
to Drive You Totally Meshuggeneh!

By PETER WEISZ

gefen
publishing house
JERUSALEM ◆ NEW YORK
Est. 1981

Typesetting: Michelle Kaplan, Renana Typesetting

ISBN: 978-965-921-5

1 3 5 7 9 8 6 4 2

Gefen Publishing House Ltd.
6 Hatzvi Street
Jerusalem 94386, Israel
972-2-538-0247
orders@gefenpublishing.com

Gefen Books
11 Edison Place
Springfield, NJ 07081
516-593-1234
orders@gefenpublishing.com

www.gefenpublishing.com

Printed in the United States

For my grandchildren.
Ezra, Zella, Benno and May

Introduction

Jews have always been a puzzling people. In both senses of the word. We have certainly caused consternation and bewilderment over the ages (just contemplate the mysteries of gefilte fish, for example). And, we have, as a people, always enjoyed a good intellectual challenge. Examples abound.

The Passover Seder comes to mind with its refrain of "Who Knows One?" in which the entire spectrum of Jewish theology is laid out in a "One-Two Buckle My Shoe" guessing game.

Jewish sacred texts, such as the Talmud, are filled with brain-benders and riddles. "How do you divide an estate so that everyone is treated fairly?" And don't get me started on gematria!

From dreidels to Dungeons & Dragons, Jews have always loved a good mental challenge. And that's why I wrote this book. It contains some of my favorite puzzles, lovingly collected over the years. Some of them I created and some I have borrowed. I've tried to give each one a bit of a Jewish twist to add to the flavor. But, like they used to say about the rye bread...

You Don't Have To Be Jewish to Enjoy This Book!

You'll notice that I've rated the difficulty of each puzzle on a one (easiest) to five (hardest) Jewish star scale.

If you have a favorite kosher-style brain-teaser, please send it to me and, if I like it, I'll include it in a future edition. Also send along any corrections you discover.

Send it to: peter@peterweisz.com with the words "Puzzle Tov" in the subject line.

Meanwhile, try your hand at these kosher conundrums and, if you do well, then congratulate yourself and say: Puzzle Tov!

Peter Weisz,
March 2017

DIFFICULTY KEY

✡ = Easy Peasy

✡ ✡ = Not too tough

✡ ✡ ✡ = Make your mother proud.

✡ ✡ ✡ ✡ = Oy! Mein Kop!

✡ ✡ ✡ ✡ ✡ = Maven level

The Rabbi's Children

My rabbi, who loves puzzles, has three children.

"How old are your children, Rabbi?" I asked him one day.

"Well, let's see if you can use your Jewish knowledge to figure it out," he replied. "The product of their ages is double-*chai*."

"So if I multiply their ages together, I'll get 36, right?" I said.

"That's right," said the rabbi.

"Well, that's not enough to go on," I complained. "What do you get if you add up their three ages?"

"You get a number that's equal to the bar mitzvah age," he said with a smile.

I thought for a second.

"Still not enough information," I said. "Tell me something more, please."

"My oldest child is left-handed."

"Aha!" I shouted. "Got it!"

How old are the rabbi's three children?

7

 page 70

The Black Hat Bargain

Shlomo's family are Chasidim. He just turned 14 and received a big black hat from his father, who happens to be a casino manager and loves to play betting games.

Shlomo has been receiving a $5 per week allowance for nearly two years. Now that he has his own black hat, he thinks that it's time for a raise and tells his Dad:

"I need to go to ten dollars per week, Abba."

After a bit of thought, his father responds:

"Well, I can't okay that, but I will make you a proposition, if you feel like taking a gamble."

"What is it this time, Abba?" Shlomo moans while rolling his eyes.

"Here's the deal. I have right here ten ten-dollar bills. And here I have ten one-dollar bills," he said, placing all twenty bills in front of Shlomo. He then took off his own black hat and placed it upside down on the table. He asked for Shlomo's new hat and did the same, placing the two hats side by side.

"Each week, and if you agree, I will give you the opportunity of distributing all twenty bills into the two hats in any way you choose. Once you've done that, you'll be blindfolded. I will then move the hats so you won't know which is on the right or on the left. It will then be your job to indicate one of the two hats by saying right or left. You then reach into the hat you have picked and draw out one, and only one, bill. Whatever you pick, you keep. Pick a ten, keep a ten. Pick a one, you get a one. *Vershtayst?*" Shlomo said he understood.

A few ground rules:
Shlomo is not permitted to fold, or otherwise attach one bill to another when he distributes the bills.

Shlomo is not permitted to mark, or in any other way alter the feel, smell, taste or sound of the bills.

Shlomo must place ALL of the bills into the hats. How many of each denomination he places into each hat is up to him, but each one of the twenty bills must be placed into one of the two hats.

Two Questions:
Without coming up with any further strategy, should Shlomo accept the proposition or should he stick with the $5 per week allowance?

Is there some way of arranging the bills so that Shlomo's chances of selecting a ten-dollar bill are increased?

page 71

The Eruv Ropes

In the old days, the gabbai was the fellow who took care of all the day-to-day business at a synagogue. Two important tasks he was responsible for was taking down the eruv rope at the end of Shabbat and for conducting the weekly Havdalah service.

The eruv is the roped off area around the synagogue, the "walled garden," in which Jews could carry things without violating the Sabbath. It was marked by a long piece of rope that was put up on Friday at sunset and taken down on Saturday also at sunset.

The gabbai had no watch or clock, but he knew that Havdalah had to start exactly 45 minutes after sunset. He also knew that if he cut a piece of the rope to a certain length and then lit the end, it would burn for exactly one hour.

The problem was that the rope didn't burn evenly. It could burn slowly for a while and then speed up and then slow down and so on. But it always took exactly one hour to burn the entire length.

The gabbai used two pieces of such rope of equal length and some matches to determine when 45 minutes had elapsed.

How did he do it?

 page 72

The Dishonest Waiter

Three mothers put on a joint birthday party for their kids at Moishe's Kosher Deli. When the waiter brought the bill, it came to exactly $300 including the tip.

Each mother pulled out a $100 bill and gave it to the waiter who turned the money in to Moishe. Moishe double-checked the bill and found that the waiter had made a mistake. The total should only have been $250.

"Here," he said to the waiter, "here's a twenty and three tens. Go give this back to the mothers and apologize that you overcharged them."

The waiter took the $50 but on the way he decided that it was just too hard to divide $50 three ways, so instead he gave each of the mothers back $10. He pocketed the remaining $20. "They'll never know the difference," he thought to himself.

Each of the mothers paid $100 and got back $10, thereby paying $90 each.

$90 times three is $270. This is the total that was paid by all three mothers.

Add this to the $20 in the waiter's pocket and you get only $290.

What happened to the missing $10?

11   💡 page 73

What's So Special?

A rabbi told his pupils to study this paragraph and all things in it:

"What is vitally wrong with it? Probably, nothing in it is truly wrong, but you must admit that it is most unusual. Don't just zip through it quickly, but study it scrupulously – just as you would do with Torah. With luck you should spot what is so particular about this paragraph and the words found in it. Can you now say what it is? If not, tax your brains and try again. Don't miss a word or a symbol. It isn't all that difficult, you know."

No pupil could do it. Can you?

The Two Rabbis

An old rabbi and a young rabbi were seated next to each other on the bimah. The young rabbi was the son of the old rabbi, but the old rabbi was not the father of the young one. How do you explain this?

page 74

The Switch Hitter

One fine day, Nate Goldstein got a call from a lawyer.

"I'm afraid I have some sad news," he said. "Your great-uncle Isadore passed away last week. You were named in the will. Could you meet me at the synagogue tomorrow morning and I'll explain?"

Nate remembered that Uncle Izzy was a wealthy man, albeit a bit eccentric. Nate agreed to meet the lawyer and arrived at the shul the next morning where the attorney told him the following:

"Your great-uncle's will contained a strange provision. He wants you to turn on this little light bulb next to his brass name plaque every year on his yahrzeit – the anniversary day of his death. For this, his estate will pay you $25,000 every year."

The lawyer showed Nate the name plate mounted on the wall of the sanctuary. Next to it was a little light bulb. It was not turned on.

"Of course," said Nate. "I'll be glad to do it. Where's the light switch?"

"That's just it," answered the lawyer. "There's a hitch."

"A hitch?"

"Yes, a hitch with the switch. Follow me." The lawyer led Nate to the Rabbi's office behind the bimah and pointed to a wall plate containing three light switches. Nate was puzzled:

"But there are three switches and I can't see the little light bulb from here. How do I know which of the switches controls the bulb?" Nate protested.

The lawyer replied: "That's the hitch. Your great-uncle wanted to make sure that whoever was going to handle this job was highly intelligent. So he devised a little test. Here's how it works:

One and only one of these three switches controls the light bulb. Right now the bulb is off and all three switches are in the OFF position. You will be able to fiddle around with the switches for five minutes. After that you will be able to go back into the sanctuary and observe the bulb. At that point, if you can identify which of the switches controls the bulb, then you get the job. $25,000 every year just to flick a switch. Are you interested?"

As Nate thought this over the lawyer explained further: "You must work alone and cannot use any equipment, such as a camera, to help you. There is no way to tell from the rabbi's office if the light is on or off. After you go in to the sanctuary and observe the bulb, you may not return to the switches. Got it?" Nate said that he understood and told the lawyer to start the clock.

After five minutes Nate was able to correctly identify which of the three switches controlled the light bulb. How did he do it?

page 75

Einstein's Candles

When Jewish physicist Albert Einstein was a seven-year-old, his Hebrew School teacher gave the class an assignment he hoped would keep all the students busy for a while.

"Boys and girls, we have been learning about Chanukah, the Festival of Lights that will soon be here. As you know, on the first night we light one candle of the menorah, two candles on the second night, and so on adding a candle each night for eight nights. In addition we also light an extra candle each night called the shamash to light the other candles with. I want you all to take a pencil and paper and add up all the candles, including the shamashes, that will be used by one menorah during the entire eight days of Chanukah."

After just five seconds, and without any written calculations, young Albert popped up with the right answer.

"How did you do it so quickly?" asked the teacher.

"I used a shortcut," he said.

The teacher immediately recognized that this kid was going to be a genius.

What is the correct answer and what was Einstein's shortcut?

15

page 76

The Bar Mitzvah Brother

Thirteen-year-old Jared stepped to the microphone to deliver his bar mitzvah speech. What he had to say shocked the congregation:

"I recently learned that I have a brother from whom I was separated at birth. I'd like you all to meet him."

Out walked another young man who looked exactly like Jared. He approached the microphone and said: "Shabbat Shalom. My name is Joel and I'm Jared's brother. Jared and I were born on the same day in the same place."

"And we have the same mother and the same father," Jared said. "But we are not twins."

How was this possible?

In The Old West

A non-observant Jewish cowboy rode into town on Shabbat. He stayed in town for three days and then rode out of town on Shabbat. How is this possible?

page 77

The Long Shofar

An American collector of ancient Judaic artifacts purchased a valuable shofar (ram's horn) at an auction in Jerusalem. When he got it back to his hotel and measured it, he discovered it was 40 inches long and realized he had a problem. He was booked to fly back to New York that evening on El Al and he knew that the airline security regulations did not permit any item on the plane, either carry-on or checked luggage, that was longer than thirty-two inches in any dimension. He also knew that the airlines strictly enforced this policy, and if he tried to violate it, the shofar would be confiscated.

He could not risk losing the shofar and he did not dare ship the valuable and fragile artifact. After a bit of thought he hit upon a solution. Making a quick stop in Tel Aviv's commercial district on his way to the airport, the collector was able to board the plane with his shofar and encountered no difficulties. He did not break the shofar into pieces or in any way alter its length. He did not bribe any of the airline security officials. He did not conceal the shofar. Yet he was able to bring the shofar home aboard the airline without violating any of the rules.

What did he stop and buy and how did he get his shofar home?

page 78

Voz Izt Vater?

Name the next letter in the series…

A B G D H V

The Hillel Hoax

The curator of the Israel Museum in Jerusalem received an excited message from an archeologist.

"We have unearthed something very valuable. It's a scroll containing the Golden Rule ('That which is hateful to you, do not do unto others…etc.'). It's signed and dated by Hillel himself." The curator asked to see it at once.

Examining the scroll very carefully, the curator could clearly make out the name Hillel, the place as Jerusalem, and the date 25 BCE. Although the date and place corresponded, the curator still rejected the scroll as a fraud and a hoax.

How did he know?

page 79

The Challah Recipe Problem

Golda has a problem. She has been asked to bake challahs for a congregational Shabbat dinner. She was given a new recipe but she doesn't have the proper culinary equipment. The recipe calls for exactly four quarts of water.

Golda has two bowls. One holds five quarts and the other holds three quarts. She has an unlimited supply of water.

How does she measure out exactly four quarts?

The *Chevra Kadisha* Riddle

The person who builds it doesn't use it. The person who buys it doesn't use it. The person who uses it doesn't know he's using it. What is it?

page 80

The *Pushke* Problem

Mr. Maven is a Sunday School teacher who loves puzzles. One Sunday he brought out four empty *pushkes* (charity collection boxes). They were labeled A, B, C, and D.

"Attention, class," he announced. "I have placed a different coin into each of these four boxes. They are a silver dollar, a half-dollar, a quarter and a dime. Your job is to guess which box contains which coin. Please write down the letters A, B, C, and D and next to each one write the value of the coin you think each box contains."

The thirty-two middle-school kids did as they were told and the papers were collected and graded by the teacher.

"Did I tell you there was a prize?" said the teacher. "It's a 2 lb. kosher salami. But it does not go to the person who got the most coins correct. Instead it will go to the person who can first answer these two questions:

"I received thirty-two answers. Of these, thirteen kids got only one coin correct and eleven kids got two coins correct. How many kids got three coins correct and how many got all four correct?"

What are the correct answers?

page 81

20

The Lost Year

A great Jewish philosopher died in 2016. He was born in Europe in 1928 and moved to the USA after World War II. He lived a full eighty-eight years. Yet his age at death was listed everywhere as eighty-seven. Why was this?

This has nothing to do with different calendars (i.e. Hebrew vs. English), customs, or leap years, etc.

page 82

The Counterfeit Coins

You have applied for a job with the Mossad, the Israeli intelligence service. In order to be accepted you must pass a test.

You are presented with ten cloth bags, each bag containing ten one-shekel coins. You are told that one of the bags contains ten counterfeit coins and the only way to tell the difference between a counterfeit and a real coin is that the counterfeit coins each weigh nine grams while the real coins each weigh ten grams. All the coins look identical.

You are provided with a scale that will display the exact weight in grams of whatever you place on the platform. But you may only use it once.

You may take the coins out of the bags and manipulate them any way you wish.

How do you determine which bag contains the counterfeit coins?

 page 83

The Let's Make a Meal Deal

Every year at Passover, my Uncle Sherman would invariably play the same game with all the kids. He would hide the afikomen (the piece of matzoh needed to complete the Seder) under one of three identical plates. The plates were numbered one, two and three and it was our job to guess which plate hid the afikomen. If we guessed correctly we received money or a gift.

He played it the same way with each kid. First the child would be asked to select a plate, but before it was turned over, my uncle would turn over ANOTHER plate that was always empty. Then he would say: "Would you like to switch plates?" and the kid could either stay with the original choice or switch.

For example, if I said I thought the afikomen was under plate number two, he might turn over plate number one to show it was not under there. Then I was given the chance to switch to plate number three, if I so chose. Or I could stick with my original choice of number two.

It seemed to me that it really didn't matter if I switched or not since I had two choices and the odds were fifty-fifty no matter which of the two plates I selected. But, after several years, I observed that the kids who said that they DID want to switch got prizes about twice as often as the kids who did not.

How do you explain this phenomenon?

 page 84

Avoiding Hamburger

In the shtetl village of Anatevka, next door to Tevye the Milkman, lived an old farmer who had three sons and seventeen cows. When the farmer died he left the cows to the sons as follows:

> The oldest son gets ½ the cows
>
> The middle son gets ⅓ of the herd
>
> The youngest son is to receive ⅑.

The sons *"dreyed their kopps"* (wracked their brains) trying to figure out how to comply with their father's wishes and determined that they would have to take all the animals to the shochet (slaughterer) and turn them into ground beef.

Fortunately, Tevye heard of their plight and offered them a suggestion that succeeded in dividing the cows to everyone's satisfaction – without resorting to hamburger.

What was Tevye's solution?

page 85

Watch Your Step

A young man meets with a rabbi to plan his bar mitzvah. The rabbi, who does not know the boy or his family, asks him several questions, such as:

"What is your Hebrew name?" and the boy answers.
"And what is your stepfather's name?"
"How did you know I have a stepfather?" asks the boy.
How did the Rabbi know?

Mixing up the Menorah

By moving only one candle, arrange this menorah so that lit and unlit candles alternate (every other candle is lit and every other candle is unlit).

page 86

Dry as a Bone

In a particular religious neighborhood in New York, every family on the block has a sukkah. One time it rained very hard, yet none of the sukkahs got wet. How come?

The Kittel Riddle

Little Bernie was boasting to Rachel that at the previous night's Passover Seder, he found the afikomen and got a big prize.

"Where did you find it?" she asked.

"In the pocket of my father's kittel," he replied.

"You're a liar!" she exclaimed and she was right. How did she know?

 page 87

The *Kippah* Conundrum

Mr. Maven, the Sunday School teacher and Puzzle Master, arrived to class with a new challenge for the boys only.

"I have in this bag ten kippot (skullcaps). Some are white and some are black," he announced.

He then instructed ten boys to line their chairs up in a row, with each boy, except for the first, seated facing the back of the boy in front of him.

Mr. Maven then placed a random *kippah* on the head of each boy. Each boy could see only the kippot on the heads in front of him. No boy could see his own *kippah* nor any behind him.

"I am going to give you ten minutes to consult. You need to come up with a team strategy that will result in at least nine of you being correct when I ask you, in order, starting from the back, to name the color of the *kippah* on your own head. I will announce if you are right or wrong as soon as you give your answer. If your team succeeds in getting nine right, each of you will receive a 2 lb. kosher salami."

After a few minutes of huddling, they came up with a plan that would guarantee nine, and possibly ten, correct answers. What was the strategy?

page 88

Movers and Shakers

My friend Abe told me the following story:

"Last night my wife, Brenda, and I attended a Jewish Federation dinner. Once there we met with four other couples. Their names were: Charlie and Denise, Ed and Francie, George and Harriet, and Irv and Janie.

We all arrived at about the same time and a round of handshaking ensued as we made our introductions.

Once we were seated at our table, my mathematical curiosity became active and I questioned each of the others about the handshaking that had just taken place. I learned the following:

No one shook hands with another person more than once.

No one shook hands with his or her own spouse.

Every person in our group reported that they shook hands with a different number of people."

Given these facts, are you able to determine how many hands were shaken by Abe's wife, Brenda?

page 90

Jewish Celebrity Name Game

All of the 22 celebrities pictured on the following pages have (or had) two things in common. They are/were Jewish and they opted to change their original birth names to ones that sound a bit less Jewish.

Try to correctly match the celebrity's original birth name found on the list provided on page 33.

Answers and scoring on the following pages.

Joan Rivers: _____   Tony Randall: _____

Dinah Shore: _____   Gene Wilder: _____

5

6

Rodney
Dangerfield: ____

Jack Benny: ____

7

8

June Allyson: ____

Woody Allen: ____

9

10

Danny Kaye: ____

Mel Brooks: ____

Cary Grant: _____   Lauren Bacall: _____

Ralph Lauren: _____   Larry King: _____

Albert Brooks: _____   Howard Cossell: _____

Michael Landon: _____

Bob Dylan: _____

George Burns: _____

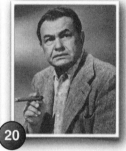

Edward G.
Robinson: _____

Jerry Lewis: _____

Kirk Douglass: _____

Birth Name List

A.	Naftali Birnbaum
B.	Howard Cohen
C.	Jack Cohen
D.	Issur Danielovitch
E.	Albert Einstein
F.	Ella Geisman
G.	Emmanuel Goldenberg
H.	David Kaminsky
I.	Melvin Kaminsky
J.	Larry Koenig
K.	Allen Koenigsberg
L.	Benny Kubelsky
M.	Larry Leach
M.	Joseph Levitch
O.	Rafael Lifshitz
P.	Joan Molinsky
Q.	Michael Orowitz
R.	Bette Persky
S.	Leonard Rosenberg
T.	Frances Rose Schorr
U.	Jerome Silverman
V.	Robert Zimmerman

page 92

Spin and Win

Dreidels have been a part of Jewish tradition for centuries. They are typically used during Chanukah as part of a game intended to remind youngsters about the meaning of the holiday. Each of the dreidel's four sides bears one of the following Hebrew letters: נ, ג, ה, ש.

The letters are the initial letters of a phrase that translates: "A Great Miracle Happened There," a reference to the Maccabees' victory that restored Jewish sovereignty in ancient Israel. It also refers to how a small amount of oil was miraculously able to illuminate the redeemed Temple for eight days.

From this we learn two things:

Dreidels have long been associated with wordplay and…

Jews have been dealing with a lack of sufficient oil in Israel for even longer.

It is in the spirit of the first point that we present the following two-part dreidel puzzle, created by noted Chicago puzzle-master (and the author's son): Sandy Weisz.

Spin and Win (cont.)

Each of the dreidels on the following page contains a four-letter word, with one letter of the word on each of the four sides. Only two of the sides are visible. Your job is to figure out each entire word using the clues below and then give the dreidel a mental 180-degree spin so the other two letters are exposed. Write those two hidden letters under the dreidel.

NOTE: *The clues are in alphabetical order. They are not in the same order as the dreidels.*

But wait, there's more! Put together all the two-letter pairs in the order they appear. This will spell out a Master Clue. If it doesn't, try reversing some of the thirteen letter pairs.

Follow the instruction of the Master Clue on the next page to find the Winning Word. Write this word at the bottom of the page in order to solve the puzzle.

Here are the clues:

Actually existing
Brainstorm output
Dreidel prize
Eat sparingly
Kind or class
Lay in the sun
Military takeover

Musical phrase
Not right
Slow-cooked dish
Soon upon us
These power a longship
Window blind piece

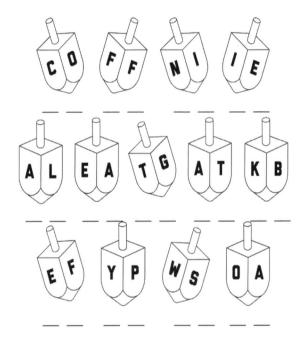

Winning Word: _____

The Amazing Number 26

The Hebrew language uses letters to signify lower number values, so that the first letter of the alphabet, Aleph, equals 1, Bet equals 2 and so on. Judaism attaches special meaning to numbers, such as 18, which stands for Life since the the two Hebrew letters that spell the word *Chai* (life) add up to 18.

The number 26 is especially noteworthy because it transcends Hebrew and also has a special meaning in English. First the Hebrew:

The four letters that spell out the ineffable name of God, YHWH (often pronounced Yahweh or Jehovah in English), when converted to numbers, total 26.

The number 26 also corresponds to the number of letters in the English alphabet. Assign the value of 1 to the letter A and number the rest, all the way to 26 for Z. Now count the number associated with the letters G, O and D. G = 7, O = 15, D = 4. The total is 26.

Hence, in both Hebrew and in English, 26 must be regarded as God's number. Here's a puzzle about this "holy" number.

Take the numbers 2, 3, 4 and 5 and the four arithmetic operators: plus, minus, multiply and divide. Using all four numbers exactly once each and using any three of the four operators exactly once each, devise a formula that will yield the number 26.

No square roots, exponents or any other types of operators permitted. The four numbers are single digit positive integers.

page 94

Birthday Brain Teaser

I ran into Sid, the wise guy, at the synagogue last September. I hadn't seen him for a while so I asked him how old he now was.

"Uh, let's see," he said, removing his *kippah* to scratch his head. "I was 32 years old the day before yesterday and I'll be 35 next year."

How was this possible?

Showdown at the Shul

It was poker night at the temple and there were six players left in the game when the clock struck midnight.

"You know it's getting late," said Murray. "Let's call it a night."

"How about a last round showdown?" suggested Fred. All six agreed.

They would all push their remaining chips into the middle of the table and deal out one card each. The player who got the highest card would take out half the pot plus one extra chip for good luck. The player with the next highest card would do the same with the remaining chips. Half the pot plus one. When they got to the sixth player, there were no chips left.

How many chips were in the pot to begin with?

 page 95

38

Bernie's Bagels

Bernie brought a basket of twelve bagels to the morning minyan service. Afterwards he gave one bagel to each of the twelve other people who attended the service, yet there was one bagel that remained in the basket.

How do you explain this?

My Three Sons

Max's mother has three sons. Her oldest is named Abraham. Her second oldest is named Isaac. What is the name of her youngest?

The Missing Mezuzah Piece

A Judaica gift shop owner has received a shipment of nine identical mezuzot. Each one is supposed to contain a parchment scroll, but she has been tipped off that one is empty. She cannot open them, so she must compare their weights to determine the light mezuzah.

She is able to discover this using a balance scale only two times. How does she do it?

 page 96

The Brooklyn Bar Bet

After attending the reading of the Megillah on Purim, Jerry and Louie stopped off at the neighborhood bar. Jerry laid out six half-dollar coins as shown below and said:

"You see that there are two rows of coins. The horizontal row has four coins and the vertical row has three. I'll bet you that I can move just one coin to make two rows with each row containing four coins. If I can't do it then you keep the coins. If I can do it, you pay me $3."

Louie took the bet but lost. How did Jerry do it?

✡ ✡ ✡

The Albatross Sandwich

A Jewish sailor goes into a restaurant that is the only one known to serve albatross sandwiches. The sailor orders one and takes a bite. He immediately smiles and rejoices. Why?

 page 97

The Kinder Cult

There once was a sect of Jews who lived on an isolated island in the Black Sea. The population consisted of 1,000 married couples. For some reason they were all unable to have children. So they sent to Israel and asked a famous rabbi to come and help them.

The rabbi arrived after Rosh Hashanah and proclaimed the following: "Beginning this year you will all be able to have one child a year. But you must follow this rule: You must have a child every year until you give birth to a boy. Once you have a son, you must stop having children. But if you give birth to a girl, you must continue each year until you have a son."

The people agreed and began the practice faithfully right away. Gender at birth was normal. On the average, half the babies born were girls, half boys.

Ten years later the rabbi returned. Because couples kept having baby girls and stopped when they had a boy, he expected to see an island overrun with young girls, but what he found surprised him.

Assuming that his instructions were followed precisely every year and that no children died, how many boys and how many girls did the rabbi observe upon his return?

 page 98

Eastside / Westside

Brenda is retired and lives in Central Park West in Manhattan. She has a grandson who lives in Newark and a granddaughter who lives in Queens. She's also something of a gambler.

Every day she goes to the subway station and catches either a train going west to Newark or one going east to Queens. She likes to leave it up to chance and gets on whichever train arrives first.

Both trains run all day and night and both stop at Brenda's station once every hour. She has noticed that no matter what time of day or night she goes to the subway station, she winds up in Newark with her grandson about ten times as often as in Queens.

She is puzzled since she randomly picks the time to enter the station, and since both trains come once every hour, she feels this method should get her to Queens about half the time and to Newark about half the time.

Why is she winding up in Newark so much more frequently?

page 99

Moses on the Mountain

Moses started traveling at sunrise up the only path to the top of Mount Sinai. He arrived to the top exactly at sunset. After spending the night in the company of the burning bush, Moses rose the next morning at sunrise and made his way back down the mountain on the same path arriving at sunset.

Moses had no way to measure his walking rate. He had no watch, clock, sundial, hourglass or other chronometer to measure the time. Yet he was convinced that he was at the exact same spot along the path at the exact same time at least one time on both days.

How could he be sure?

43

page 100

The Smart Spot Puzzle

An elderly rebbe was approached by his three top students. Avrum, Berel, and Gedalia.

"Which one of us is the smartest?" they all three asked of him.

"As it says in the Book of Proverbs," replied the wise man, "Fear of the Lord is the beginning of wisdom."

He then instructed the young men to sit in a circle facing each other and to close their eyes.

"Let's do a little test," the rebbe said. "I'm going to paint a dot on each of your foreheads. The dot will either be red or blue. When I say 'Open,' you will all three open your eyes. If you see a red dot on either of the other two, you should raise your hand. The first one of you who correctly can tell me the color of the dot on his own forehead will be declared the smartest. Understood?" All three nodded and then closed their eyes as the rebbe put either a red dot or a blue dot on each of their foreheads.

"Open!" the rebbe announced.

All three quickly opened their eyes and immediately all raised their hands. They sat pondering for a few moments until finally Avrum announced: "I have a red dot."

"Correct and Mazel Tov!" said the rebbe.

How did Avrum know?

 page 101

The Clever Mikvah Guide

An American Orthodox rabbi was leading a group of his lady congregants on a tour of the Jewish Quarter of Jerusalem.

"Ladies," he announced, "this morning, in preparation for Shabbat, we will visit an ancient mikvah (ritual bath) and you will all be able to participate."

When the group arrived, the tourist guide explained that the mikvah was very old and fragile and therefore had a weight limit.

"Can you tell me the total weight of your group?" the guide quietly asked the rabbi.

"I don't know," he replied, "and I'm not about to ask them their weights. Some of these ladies are very sensitive about that subject."

"Hold on," said the guide. "I know just what to do. Please introduce me to the women." The rabbi did so as the group was seated around a conference table in a meeting room next to the mikvah. The guide passed out pencils and slips of paper to all the women.

He next wrote something on a slip of paper and handed it to the first lady as he whispered something in her ear. The lady then looked at the slip she had received and then wrote something on another slip of paper. This she handed to the woman on her left. At this point, the guide whispered the same instruction to the second lady. This went on around the table until the last woman handed her slip back to the guide.

The guide looked at the paper and immediately knew the total weight of the group with full privacy preserved. He did not learn the weight of any of the women. None of the women learned the weight of any of the others as well.

How did he know the total weight and what did he instruct the ladies to do in order to accomplish this?

page 103

The Frigid Digits

The Lubavitch movement, also known as Chabad, is renowned for establishing houses of Jewish worship in some of the world's most remote locations. Among these is the little community of Alcan in the Yukon that sits right on the Alaska / Canada border.

One day the senior rabbi asked the junior rabbi to post a sign in the synagogue.

"It's going to be a very cold winter," the elder clergyman explained. "I don't want people trying to come to the shul when it's too cold outdoors. *Pikuach nefesh* must take precedence."

The rabbi was referring to the Jewish teaching that it is permitted to violate commandments, such as coming to the synagogue on the Sabbath, in order to preserve or promote one's health.

"What should the sign say?" asked the younger rabbi.

"It should read: 'When the outdoor temperature is below this number, please stay at home and do not come to the synagogue.'" The older rabbi then told him the number.

"Remember, Rabbi," said the younger man, "that about half of our congregants live in Alaska and they use the English system and the other half are Canadians who use the metric system. So you should indicate if the temperature is in Fahrenheit or Celsius."

"In this case," replied the wise elder, "it doesn't matter."

What temperature was displayed on the sign?

Two-by-Two

How many animal species did Moses take with him on the Ark?

page 105

Bagels and Bialys

Tammy applied for her first job at the local kosher bakery. "Do you know the difference between a bagel and bialy?" asked the owner.

"Sure," answered Tammy. "A bialy doesn't have a hole."

"Correct," said the owner. "Now here's a little test. See those three boxes? One contains bagels, one contains bialys and the third contains both. Each box has a sign on it that is supposed to identify the contents, but all three signs are wrong. You are permitted to reach in blindly and take one item out of any one box that you choose. At that point you should be able to correctly label all three boxes."

Tammy reached in and took out one item and then was able to place all three signs correctly.

How did she do it?

page 105

The Beard Barber

Among the Chasidic sect known as the Lubavitchers, it is forbidden for men to cut their beards in any way and at any time.

In a certain Lubavitch community, a particularly strict rabbi arose to become the leader. His first decree was that, in order to make sure that no one cut his beard, each man was required to report to the official barber on the first day of each month to have his beard measured. Any reduction in beard length would be reported to the rabbi and the beard-trimmer would be expelled from the community.

It was further decreed that no one was allowed to measure his own beard. Only the official barber was permitted to do the measuring.

So...who measured the barber's beard?

51

page 106

Totaling the Ties

Shmuel the Statistician loves two things: statistics and soccer…or, as they call it everywhere except in the US…football.

Last year Shmuel attended every single IFA (Israeli Football Association) game. He rooted for the Blue and Whites as they faced off against FIFA teams from around the world. He noticed, however, that there seemed to be an inordinate number of times when the score was tied. He wondered if this was something unusually characteristic of the Israeli team, so he set off to find out.

Shmuel examined every one of the 853 matches played by the 31 FIFA teams that year and noted all the tie scores he found.

During what percentage of all soccer matches played last year was the score tied at least one time?

page 107

Dinner for Three

An observant Jewish man is seated between two non-Jewish people he does not know. All three are served a kosher dinner. After the meal, the woman to his right indicates she wishes to use the bathroom. All three stand up. After she returns they all sit down and within ten minutes, all three are asleep in their chairs.

Where did this strange meal take place?

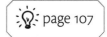

page 107

The Prime Minister Puzzle

The Supreme Court of Israel is made up of fifteen justices who are appointed by the Judicial Selection Committee.

Benjamin Netanyahu has served as Prime Minister of Israel longer than any other person and, not surprisingly, a high number of Supreme Court Justices (6 as of 1/1/17) have been appointed during his two tenures.

But he does not hold the record. See if you can guess during which Israeli Prime Minister's term or terms in office Israel saw the highest number of Supreme Court Justices appointed to the court. Here is a list of Prime Ministers:

Benjamin Netanyahu

Ehud Olmert

Ariel Sharon

Ehud Barak

Shimon Peres

Yitzhak Rabin

Yitzhak Shamir

Menachem Begin

Golda Meir

Yigal Allon

Levi Eshkol

Moshe Sharett

David Ben-Gurion

 page 108

Teller's Formula

It was claimed that Edward Teller, the famous Jewish physicist and father of the hydrogen bomb, would present the following problem to prospective candidates at the Manhattan Project to determine if they were adept at thinking "outside the box."

Can you solve it? Solve for "?".

$$(x - a)^2 \cdot (x - b)^2 \cdot (x - c)^2 \ldots (x - z)^2 = ?$$

NOTES: *"•" means multiply. There is one and only one correct answer and it is an integer.*

page 108

Flipping Coins

It was the 100th graduating class at a famous European rabbinic seminary and the school was about to ordain 100 new rabbis. The chief rabbi wanted to learn which of the graduates was the smartest, so he devised a test.

He placed 100 gold coins in a long row covering a long table. All the coins were faced heads up. He then lined up all the graduates. The chief rabbi instructed the first graduate as follows:

"Graduate number one, I want you to go down the row of coins turning every one over so that each one is tails up." He then turned to Graduate number two.

"Graduate number two, I want you to go to every other coin, starting with coin number two, and flip each of them again so that every other coin will now be heads up." Moving on to graduate number three:

"You will start with coin number three and flip it over. You will then proceed to every third coin and do the same. If the coin is heads up you will flip it so it is tails up and vice versa." The fourth graduate was instructed to do the same to every fourth coin, and so on all the way to the 100th graduate (who only had one coin to flip).

"Whoever among you is the first to correctly tell me how many coins will be heads up and how many will be tails up after the whole process is over, will receive all 100 gold coins," pronounced the chief rabbi.

What are the correct answers? How many heads up coins and how many tails up coins will there be at the end and why?

page 109

Gender Mind Bender

Moishe has two children.

"Are they boys or girls?" I asked him.

"Well," he answered, always the chochem, "the chances that the older one is a girl are $5/10$, right?"

"Right," I said, playing along.

"And the younger one? Also a $5/10$ chance that it's a girl?"

"Correct," I said.

"Okay," Moishe said. "Now I'm going to tell you something. One of my kids IS a girl. Now what are the odds that the other one is also a girl?"

Nu? What are they?

The Hay and the Horse

In Yiddish folklore the people of the mythical town of Chelm were known for their ingenious stupidity. This riddle illustrates the concept.

A farmer had a horse that was tied to a ten-foot rope. One evening he placed a bale of hay eleven feet away from the horse, yet when he returned to the corral the following morning, the horse had eaten all the hay.

How was this possible?

 page 112

The Cake and The Kinder

A young mother came to the rabbi with a problem.

"In the past, when I baked a cake," the woman explained, "I would let my two kids decide how to split the cake evenly between the two of them. I gave one the knife and said: 'Okay, you divide the cake in two and your sibling will pick which piece to take.' One cuts and the other one picks. This way there is no argument about who got the bigger piece."

"Very wise," said the Rabbi. "So what's the problem?"

"My baby now wants cake, too," she explained. "So now I have to divide the cake three ways fairly so no one feels they got short-changed. I have to figure out some rules that will make sure that happens. And the rules have to work even if two of the kids try to make a secret deal to short-change the third one. It has to be collusion-proof."

After some thought, the Rabbi came up with a solution. What was it?

page 113

Running in the Rain

Five men were outdoors crossing a large yard together. Suddenly it began to rain. No one had an umbrella. Four of the five men began walking faster, but the fifth did not. Surprisingly, the four men who sped up all got wet, while the fifth man remained dry. How do you account for this?

Getting Off the Island

In ancient Judea, there was an island in the Sea of Galilee located not far from the mainland. The island was ruled by an evil king who did not permit any of his subjects to leave the island under penalty of death. He also required that anyone coming onto the island from the mainland pay a hefty toll tax.

The only way to get on or off the island was via a foot-bridge that took exactly eight minutes to cross.

The king built a guardhouse on the island side of the bridge that was staffed around the clock with a single guard. Once inside the guardhouse, the guard could not observe the bridge. Each guard was required to follow the following rules:

Anyone observed crossing from the island to the mainland must be shot on sight.

Anyone coming to the island from the mainland must pay 1,000 shekels or be sent back.

The guard must come out of the guardhouse every five minutes and observe the bridge for a full minute before returning.

A clever Hebrew fellow figured out how to escape the island. How did he do it?

page 115

The Busy Bulbul Bird

Before World War II, the towns of Minsk and Pinsk, located exactly 300 km apart in what is today Belarus, were vibrant centers of Jewish culture. The tiny village of Slutsk is situated almost precisely between the two towns.

One day, the only Jewish schoolteacher in Slutsk directed his class's attention to one of the many beautiful bulbul birds that inhabited the nearby woods.

"The bulbul bird is very fast flyer," the teacher explained to his students. "I'll give you an example.

"Yesterday, at 12 noon, a train began traveling from Minsk on a straight track to Pinsk. At the exact same moment another train began going the other way on the adjoining track from Pinsk to Minsk.

"At the exact moment that the first train left the Minsk station a bulbul bird took off from its locomotive and flew along the track straight towards Pinsk. When it met the second train, the bird turned around 180 degrees and began flying back towards the first train. When it reached the first train, it again turned tail and flew back to the second. It continued going back and forth in this way until the two trains met.

"If the first train was traveling at a constant speed of 100 km per hour, and…

"If the second train was traveling at a constant speed of 50 km per hour, and…

"If the bulbul bird was traveling at a constant speed of 150 km per hour…

"And assuming the bird switched direction instantly each time it met one of the trains, how many kilometers did the bulbul bird cover by the time the two trains met?"

page 116

Dominos and Chess

Chess is known in some quarters as "The Jewish National Game," with dominos a close second. A currently active Jewish chess champion from Hungary, Judith Polgar, is considered the greatest female chess player of all time.

Not long ago, Judith was challenged by a male chess colleague who asked her to solve the following puzzle:

The challenger laid out a standard chessboard and then removed exactly 31 random dominos from the box. When a domino was placed onto the chessboard, it covered exactly two squares.

"By placing these 31 dominos on the chessboard, you will be able to cover 62 of the 64 squares, leaving two uncovered. Can you arrange the dominos so that the two remaining uncovered squares are at the opposite corners of the board?"

"Of course not," Judith exclaimed instantly. "I can't do it and neither can you, nor can anyone else. It's impossible."

How did she know?

page 117

From the Balcony

Orthodox synagogues have a barrier, known as a "mechitzah," that separates male from female worshippers. Some (especially Sephardi Jews) place the women's area upstairs in a balcony overlooking the men's seating area.

Mrs. Nussbaum was upstairs in the women's section and trying to make out the seat number that her husband below was occupying. The seat numbers were painted on the floor in front of each seat and Mr. Nussbaum was blocking her view of the number of his seat. Also, the seat numbers seemed to be very oddly arranged.

Can you help her identify the seat number Mr. Nussbaum is in?

page 118

Pita Party Puzzle

It was Nadav's eighth birthday and his mother took him and his seven friends to their favorite restaurant and ordered a big plate of humous for them.

"Where's the pita?" cried Nadav when the humous arrived.

"I'm sorry," said the waiter, "but we only have two pieces left." He presented the two large pieces of pita bread.

"But we have eight children," said Nadav's mother. "Can you cut them into eight pieces?"

"Yes," said the waiter, "but we charge one shekel per cut."

"I only have two shekels left," said Nadav's mother. "What will I do?"

Nadav popped up with: "I know. I can make eight pieces, all the same size, with only two cuts."

How did he do it?

page 119

Equation Occasion

Numbers have special meanings in Judaism. For example, in the equation below, the first number, five, stands for the Five Books of Moses contained in the Torah, or holy scroll. The second number, three, refers to the three patriarchs in the Torah: Abraham, Isaac and Jacob. The number 70 refers to the year 70 CE when the Romans destroyed the Second Temple. And the number 613 is equal to the number of total commandments found in the Torah.

There's only one problem. The equation is not correct. Other than drawing a slanted line across the equals sign, can you make the equation correct by adding just one straight-line stroke?

$$5 + 3 + 70 = 613$$

page 120

Solutions

THE RABBI'S CHILDREN

Since multiplying the ages yields a product of 36, here are all eight possible combinations:

$$1 \times 1 \times 36 = 36 \qquad 1 \times 6 \times 6 = 36$$
$$1 \times 2 \times 18 = 36 \qquad 2 \times 2 \times 9 = 36$$
$$1 \times 3 \times 12 = 36 \qquad 2 \times 3 \times 6 = 36$$
$$1 \times 4 \times 9 = 36 \qquad 3 \times 3 \times 4 = 36$$

How many of these factors of 36 add up to 13? Exactly two:

$$2 + 2 + 9 = 13$$
$$1 + 6 + 6 = 13$$

(NOTE: *Even if you don't know that the bar mitzvah age is 13, you can figure this out since 13 is the only sum of the factors that appears twice. If it didn't, we would not need further information and could figure out the ages at this point.*)

But we still don't know which is correct until the rabbi says: "My OLDEST (not older) CHILD (not children) is left-handed."

If there is an oldest child that means that only the 2, 2, 9 combination can be correct.

ANSWER: 2, 2, 9.

THE BLACK HAT BARGAIN

The answer to the first question is YES. Since, if he distributes the bills randomly, each week Shlomo will have a 50% chance of drawing either a ten-dollar or a one-dollar bill, his expectation will be the average of those two amounts. $10 + $1 / 2 = $5.50.

That's 50 cents more per week than he is currently receiving.

But what if he distributed the bills more intelligently? For example, let's say he places nine ten-dollar bills into one hat and added in all the one-dollar bills. He places the remaining ten-dollar bill into the other hat.

In this way he has a 50% chance of getting the single ten-dollar bill each week. On the other weeks, he has a 9 out of 19 or 47.4% chance of getting a tenner.

If after half the hat pulls Shlomo gets a ten, and if after the other half he gets a ten 47.4% of the time, then you add these two values together: 50% plus 23.7% (half of 47.4%), and Shlomo will have an expectation of collecting an average of 73.7% of $10, or $7.37, each week if he uses this method.

And that's pretty good.

THE ERUV ROPES

The gabbai lit both ends of the first piece of rope and only one end of the second piece all at the same time.

When the first rope had burned completely, he knew that one half hour had elapsed.

He, at that point, lit the unlit end of the second rope. When the second rope burned down completely, another 15 minutes (half of 30 minutes) had elapsed.

At this point a total of 45 minutes had elapsed and it was time for Havdalah.

THE DISHONEST WAITER

There is no missing $10! This is a case of misdirection. If you are attempting to account for the disposition of the $300 there is no logical reason to add the $20 in the waiter's pocket to the $270 paid out by the mothers.

Here is the correct accounting breakdown…

Of the $300 total originally paid out by the mothers:

Moishe wound up with $250

The mothers (combined) wound up with $30

And the waiter wound up with $20.

Total = $300.

WHAT'S SO SPECIAL?

You should be able to solve this one with ease. Except that there are no E's. That's right. E is the most popular letter in the English language, but it does not appear even a single time in this paragraph.

THE TWO RABBIS

The old rabbi was the young rabbi's mother.

THE SWITCH HITTER

Nate numbered the switches 1, 2, and 3. He placed both switch No.1 and switch No. 2 into the ON position.

He waited five minutes and then turned switch No. 2 to the OFF position. He then entered the sanctuary.

If the light bulb was burning, then he knew it was switch No. 1 that controlled it.

And if it was not burning, he would touch the bulb to see if it was warm.

If it was warm, then it was controlled by switch No. 2. If it was cold, which it was, then it was controlled by switch No. 3.

EINSTEIN'S CANDLES

Einstein looked at the number of candles used on the first night, which is two, as well as the number of candles used on the last night, which is nine. He then took the average of these two numbers:

$(2 + 9) / 2 = 5.5$

So the average number of candles used on any given night is 5.5. Since the interval between nights was consistent, he could multiply the average by the number of nights to get the total:

$8 \times 5.5 = 44$

ANSWER: 44 candles

THE BAR MITZVAH BROTHER

Jared and Joel are two-thirds of a set of triplets.

IN THE OLD WEST

Shabbat was the name of the cowboy's horse.

THE LONG SHOFAR

The collector purchased on old-fashioned rectangular suitcase. The dimensions of the suitcase were 32 in. by 24 in.

He placed the shofar into the suitcase diagonally, as shown.

$32^2 = 1024 \quad 24^2 = 576$

$1024 + 576 = 1600$

$\sqrt{1600} = 40$

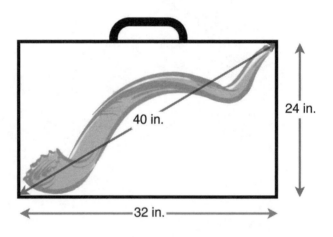

40 in.

24 in.

32 in.

VOZ IZT VATER?

The next letter is Z. The series consists of the initial letters of the names of the Hebrew alphabet letters:

Aleph, Bet, Gimmel, Daled, Hay, Vav, Zayin…

THE HILLEL HOAX

The curator knew that the letters BCE stood for "Before Common Era" or "Before Christ." This dating system did not come into being until hundreds of years after Christ. Hence, authentic documents from this period could not possibly bear such a date.

THE CHALLAH RECIPE PROBLEM

Golda fills the five quart bowl and then pours the contents into the three quart bowl, leaving behind two quarts.

Then she empties the three quart bowl.

Next, she pours the two quarts of water from the five quart bowl into the three quart bowl.

She then refills the five quart bowl.

Finally, she pours the water from the five quart bowl into the three quart bowl until it is filled. This will remove exactly one quart from the five quart bowl and leave four quarts behind.

THE *CHEVRA KADISHA* RIDDLE

The name of this riddle is a hint. The correct answer is: a coffin.

The *chevra kadisha* is the traditional Jewish burial society.

THE *PUSHKE* PROBLEM

Eight kids, 32 minus 24 (13 + 11), got all four coins correctly placed and none of the kids got three correct since it is impossible to get exactly three right. If a student gets three coins right, the fourth coin, by necessity, must also be right.

THE LOST YEAR

The key to the solution here is not *when* the philosopher was born, but *where*. It seems he died three hours before his eighty-eighth birthday…in America. But he was born in Romania, whose time zone is six hours ahead of New York's.

So at the time he died, it was already the next day – his birthday – at the place where he was born. Hence, he lived eighty eight complete years, but his death certificate read: Age at Death: eighty-seven.

THE COUNTERFEIT COINS

Number the bags 1 through 10. Take one coin from bag number 1, two coins from bag number 2, all the way to ten coins from bag number 10. You will now have fifty-five coins.

Take all fifty-five coins you have removed from the bags and place them all on the scale together.

If all the coins had all been genuine, they would each weigh ten grams and the scale would read 550 grams. But it doesn't. It shows something less than 550 grams.

If the total weight shown is one gram less than 550 (549), that tells you that you put exactly one counterfeit coin on the scale. And that means that bag number one is the bag containing the nine-gram counterfeits.

If the total weight is two grams less than 550 grams (548 grams), then bag number two contains the nine-gram counterfeits.

Etc.

THE LET'S MAKE A MEAL DEAL

The best way to understand this is to realize that when Uncle Sherman turns over an empty plate, he knows where the afikomen is located. And by revealing an empty plate, he is giving us a clue. The addition of this clue changes the odds so that it now becomes twice as likely that the afikomen is under the remaining plate that we did NOT originally pick.

The table below lists all the possibilities when the afikomen has been placed under plate number one. It shows that when the player switches (bottom half) he or she will win two out of three times. When the player does not switch he or she will win only one out of three times.

A similar table may be shown for when the afikomen is under plate number two and under plate number three, but the probabilities will remain constant.

A player will double his or her chances of winning by switching.

Afikomen Under Plate #	I select Plate No.	Do I switch?	Win or Lose?
1	1	No	Win
1	2	No	Lose
1	3	No	Lose
1	1	Yes	Lose
1	2	Yes	Win
1	3	Yes	Win

AVOIDING HAMBURGER

Since Tevye's motto was "To Life," he loaned the boys one of his cows, bringing the cow count up to eighteen, a number that symbolizes Life.

They then could do the math easily. The oldest son got ½ of the now eighteen cows, or nine cows. The middle son received ⅓ or six cows, and the youngest got ⅑ or two cows. This added up to seventeen cows and Tevye took his cow back home.

Not exactly kosher, but everyone was happy. Especially the cows.

WATCH YOUR STEP

The young man's Hebrew name was Shmuel ben Shmuel, which means Samuel son of Samuel. Since the rabbi knew that he was Ashkenazi and would not, according to custom, be named after a living relative, the rabbi concluded that the boy's father must have died before the boy was born.

The rabbi correctly assumed that the man bringing the boy to the meeting was his stepfather.

MIXING UP THE MENORAH

Pick up candle number two and use it to light candle number five. Then blow out candle number two and replace it.

DRY AS A BONE

The rain shower did not occur during Sukkoth. All the sukkahs were stored in their respective garages.

THE KITTEL RIDDLE

The kittel is white ritual robe worn by a man when he gets married, on Yom Kippur, when he leads a Seder, and when he is buried.

The kittel has no pockets because it is believed that at those times you have no need for personal possessions.

THE *KIPPAH* CONUNDRUM

They agreed that the first boy to be asked, seated in the last (number ten) seat, would shout out "White" if the total number of white kippot he saw was even. But if he saw an odd number of white kippot, he would shout out "Black."

The boy in seat number nine would pay attention if number ten was deemed correct or not. In other words, if number ten shouted out "White" and the teacher said "Wrong," then number nine now knew that number ten's *kippah* was in fact black. Combining this information with a count of the kippot in front of him, plus knowing that number ten saw an even number of white kippot, he can thereby deduce the color of his own *kippah*. In the same way each subsequent student can do the same.

Here's an example: Boy number ten sees six white kippot and three black kippot on the heads of the nine boys in front of him. So when asked what color *kippah* he is wearing, boy number ten shouts out "White," because six is an even number.

Mr. Maven says: "Wrong."

Therefore, number nine now knows that number ten's *kippah* is black.

Number nine looks at the other eight students and observes that he spots five white kippot and three black kippot. He knows that there must be an even number of white kippot, and he knows that number ten's *kippah* was black, so therefore his own *kippah* must be white.

He announces "White" and Mr. Maven says: "You're right."

Armed with this information, student number eight is able to likewise deduce the color of his own *kippah* and so on up the line.

MOVERS AND SHAKERS

This solution requires several leaps of logic. It is best presented as a Socratic dialogue in Q. and A. format:

Q. What is the highest number of hands a guest could have shaken?

A. Eight, since there were ten people and no one shook hands with himself or with his/her spouse.

Q. What is the lowest number?

A. Zero. So, other than Abe, each guest – including his wife, Brenda – shook 8, 7, 6, 5, 4, 3, 2, 1 or 0 hands. This covers all the possibilities.

Q. Was Abe's number of handshakes unique?

A. No. It couldn't be. Since all possible unique numbers have been exhausted, Abe had to have shaken hands the same number of times as one of the other guests.

Q. One of the guests shook eight hands. Let's call him Mr. Eight. Who are the guests with whom Mr. Eight did NOT shake hands?

A. There are three. Himself. His spouse. And the guest who shook zero hands. But wait. That leaves only seven people with whom he DID shake hands! Something's wrong here. Clearly two of the three people with whom Mr. Eight *did not* shake hands must be the same person.

Q. Can't Mr. Eight be the zero guest?

A. No. He shook hands with eight people.

Q. So who is the zero guest?

A. That leaves only one possibility. His wife must be the zero guest.

Q. So Mr. Eight is married to Mrs. Zero. What about the other guests?

A. By extension and using the same logic, you can deduce that Mrs. Seven is married to Mr. One. Mr. Six to Mrs. Two, etc. Actually, the gender doesn't matter. What matters is that the total sum of all hands shaken by each couple must always total eight.

Q. What are the five additive factors of the number eight?

A. 8 and 0, 7 and 1, 6 and 2, 5 and 3, 4 and 4.

Q. In which factor pair are both numbers the same?

A. 4 and 4.

Q. Who is the only guest whose handshake number matches one of the other guests?

A. Abe.

Therefore, since Abe and Brenda's handshake total must equal eight and since Abe's handshake number cannot be unique, it follows that they both shook exactly four hands.

FINAL ANSWER: Four.

JEWISH CELEBRITY NAME GAME

ANSWERS

1	Joan Rivers	P.	Joan Molinsky
2	Tony Randall	S.	Leonard Rosenberg
3	Dinah Shore	T.	Frances Rose Schorr
4	Gene Wilder	U.	Jerome Silberman
5	Rodney Dangerfield	C.	Jack Cohen
6	Jack Benny	L.	Benny Kubelsky
7	June Allyson	F.	Ella Geisman
8	Woody Allen	K.	Allen Koenigsberg
9	Danny Kaye	H.	David Kaminsky
10	Mel Brooks	I.	Melvin Kaminsky
11	Cary Grant	M.	Larry Leach
12	Lauren Bacall	R.	Bette Persky
13	Ralph Lauren	O.	Rafael Lifshitz
14	Larry King	J.	Larry Koenig
15	Albert Brooks	E.	Albert Einstein
16	Howard Cossell	B.	Howard Cohen
17	Michael Landon	Q.	Michael Orowitz
18	Bob Dylan	V.	Robert Zimmerman
19	George Burns	A.	Naftali Birnbaum
20	Edward G. Robinson	G.	Emmanuel Goldenberg
21	Jerry Lewis	N.	Joseph Levitch
22	Kirk Douglas	D.	Issur Danielovitch

SCORING:

20 to 22 correct: Cultural Maven

16 to 19 correct: Respectable.

12 to 15 correct: So-So

8 to 11 correct: Better luck next time.

7 or fewer correct: Thanks for giving it a go.

SPIN AND WIN

Military takeover: COUP	Hidden letters: UP
Musical phrase: RIFF	Hidden letters: RI
Soon upon us: NIGH	Hidden letters: GH
Eat sparingly: DIET	Hidden letters: TD
Actually existing: REAL	Hidden letters: RE
Brainstorm output: IDEA	Hidden letters: ID
Dreidel prize: GELT	Hidden letters: EL
Window blind piece: SLAT	Hidden letters: SL
Lay in the sun: BASK	Hidden letters: AS
Not right: LEFT	Hidden letters: TL
Kind or class: TYPE	Hidden letters: ET
Slow-cooked dish: STEW	Hidden letters: TE
They power a longship: OARS	Hidden letters: RS

The hidden letters, in order, spell out the following Master Clue:

UPRIGHT DREIDELS LAST LETTERS

Follow this clue to combine the last letter of the word found on each of the upright (*not tilted*) dreidels (*bold-faced above*) to get the yummy final solution:

LATKES

THE AMAZING NUMBER 26

This puzzle causes consternation because 26 has only four positive integer factors: 1, 2, 13 and 26. Only one of these, 2, is among the four numbers we are given to work with.

And if we are to reach 26 using these small numbers, then multiplication will have to enter into it somehow.

Solving this puzzle requires a certain leap of insight. You might even call it an epiphany. And here it is:

Just because the original four numbers are positive integers and the final number is a positive integer, that does not mean that all the intervening or intermediate numbers need to be positive integers. In fact, they are not.

Here is the solution:

1. Divide 3 by 2 to get 1.5
2. Add the 5 to 1.5 to get 6.5
3. Multiply 6.5 by 4 to get 26

$$((3/2)+5) \cdot 4 = 26$$

(NOTE: *The dot in the above formula indicates multiplication.*)

BIRTHDAY BRAIN TEASER

Sid, an observant Jew, went by the Hebrew calendar. His birthday fell on Erev Rosh Hashanah. That is, the day before the Jewish New Year. I met him on Rosh Hashanah of this year and so…

The day before his birthday, he was 32.

On his birthday, the last day of the previous year, he turned 33.

We met on the first day of this year.

On the last day of this year, he will turn 34.

On the last day of next year, he will turn 35.

SHOWDOWN AT THE SHUL

There were 62 chips in the pot to begin with.

The first player removed 32, leaving 30.

The second removed 16, leaving 14.

The third removed 8, leaving 6.

The fourth removed 4, leaving 2.

The fifth removed 2, leaving 0.

BERNIE'S BAGELS

Bernie gave Maxine the basket along with her bagel. He had borrowed the basket from her and was now returning it.

MY THREE SONS

Max.

THE MISSING MEZUZAH PIECE

The gift shop owner divides the mezuzot into three groups of three. She puts Group 1 and Group 2 on the scale. If they balance, then Group 3 contains the light mezuzah. If they do not balance, she knows that the lighter group on the scale contains the light mezuzah.

She then takes the group containing the light mezuzah and numbers the mezuzot 1, 2 and 3. She weighs No.1 against No. 2. If they balance, the light mezuzah is No.3. If they do not, then it's the lighter of the two on the scale.

THE BROOKLYN BAR BET

Jerry picked up coin number four and placed it on top of coin number two.

THE ALBATROSS SANDWICH

The sailor was an observant Jew who had recently been shipwrecked on a desert island with one other sailor. Before long they found they were starving, so they began hunting the island for food. The only two animals they were able to capture were a wild pig and an albatross.

The sailor explained that he would rather not eat the pig meat since it was not kosher, but he would do so if he had to, since according to the principle of *pikuach nefesh*, he was permitted to eat non-kosher food if his health depended on it.

They decided to cook the meat from the two animals using separate pots. Once the food was prepared, they could not tell which was which by appearance. They flipped a coin to decide which sailor would eat from which pot and they thereby survived.

After being rescued, the Jewish sailor searched until he found a restaurant where he could order albatross meat. After one bite he realized happily that he had eaten it before on the island and had not violated the laws of kashruth by eating pork.

THE KINDER CULT

The rabbi found an equal number of boys and girls. Nine hundred and ninety-nine of each. The fact is that practicing birth control in no way affects the gender distribution at birth.

The following table provides the year-by-year breakdown:

	No. of couples who had a baby	Boys born	Girls born
Year 1	1000	500	500
Year 2	500	250	250
Year 3	250	125	125
Year 4	125	63	62
Year 5	62	31	31
Year 6	31	15	16
Year 7	16	8	8
Year 8	8	4	4
Year 9	4	2	2
Year 10	2	1	1
Total:		**999**	**999**

EASTSIDE / WESTSIDE

The answer is in the train schedule. The train to Newark arrives at Brenda's station every hour at five minutes after the hour. The train to Queens arrives at ten minutes after the hour. The only way she will wind up on the Queens train – since she always takes the first train to arrive – is if she happens to arrive to the station between five and ten minutes after the hour.

If she arrives at any other time, the Newark train will arrive first. She only has a 12 in 1 chance of getting on the Queens train.

MOSES ON THE MOUNTAIN

Imagine that there were two Moseses. One at the top of the mountain and a second Moses at the bottom. They both begin walking on the path at sunrise at the same time, one going up, the other coming down. It follows, then, that at some point they will meet. At that point they will both be at the same place at the same time.

The fact that a twenty-four hour period elapses between the up journey and the down journey does not change the fact that the Yesterday Moses and the Today Moses had to be at the same exact spot at the same exact time.

THE SMART SPOT PUZZLE

Let's consider each possible situation that Avrum could have encountered:

1. Avrum could not have seen two blue dots. If he had, he would not have raised his hand. So that's out.

2. Avrum could have seen that Beryl had a red dot and that Gedalia had a blue dot (or vice versa). Since all three raised their hands, that means that neither of the other two saw two blue dots. Since Beryl could not have seen two blue dots, that means he saw one blue dot (on Gedalia) and one red dot (on Avrum). So, if Avrum sees a red dot and a blue dot – and since all three raised their hands – he knows that he himself must have a red dot.

3. Avrum sees two red dots. This could mean one of two things:

   a. All three dots are red, including his own or

   b. He has a blue dot.

If Avrum can rule out this last possibility, then he knows his dot must be red. Can he rule it out? Yes. Here's how:

He knows that Beryl and Gedalia are smart. If either of them sees a red dot and a blue dot on the other two, they would be able to figure out that their dot was red by the same logic as explained in No. 2 above.

Since neither one offered an answer after a few minutes had elapsed, Avrum determined that neither one sees a red dot and a blue dot. They both see two red dots. He can rule out 3b and announce that he has a red dot. As do the other two.

THE CLEVER MIKVAH GUIDE

The guide wrote down a random 3-digit number on the first slip of paper. He instructed the first woman to add her weight to this number and write the total on another slip that she should pass to her neighbor.

He instructed each woman in the same way. When the guide received the final slip, the number represented the total weight of all the women plus the original 3-digit number. The guide merely subtracted his original random number to get the total weight. And nobody learned anyone else's weight.

THE FRIGID DIGITS

Here is what the sign said:

When the outdoor temperature is below -40 degrees, please stay at home and do not come to the synagogue.

The sign does not have to specify Fahrenheit or Celsius because −40 degrees F = −40 degrees C.

TWO-BY-TWO

Zero. That was Noah, not Moses.

BAGELS AND BIALYS

Tammy reached into the box labeled "Bagels and Bialys." If she pulled out a bagel, she knew that the box contained only bagels. If she pulled out a bialy, she knew the box contained only bialys.

She next swapped the "Bagels and Bialys" sign and the sign corresponding to the item she pulled out. If she pulled out a bagel, for example, she switched the "Bagels" sign with the "Bagels and Bialys" sign.

Finally, she switched the remaining two "non-Bagel" signs. For example:

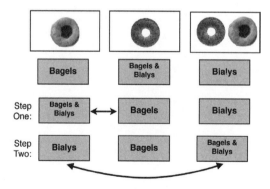

THE BEARD BARBER

No one. The barber was a woman.

TOTALING THE TIES

100%. Every game started with the score tied at 0–0.

DINNER FOR THREE

Aboard an El Al night flight from New York to Tel Aviv.

THE PRIME MINISTER PUZZLE

David Ben-Gurion. Since he was Israel's first Prime Minister, all fifteen justices were appointed during his term of office.

TELLER'S FORMULA

The answer lies in the ellipsis (the three dots representing all the terms that are not shown in the formula). We see that the second value in each term is a consecutive letter of the alphabet.

Working from the last term $(x - z)^2$ backwards, we see that the next to the last term is $(x - y)^2$ and the one before that is $(x - x)^2$, which must equal zero.

Any value multiplied by zero equals zero. Hence, the correct answer must be zero.

FLIPPING COINS

The first step is to understand that if an even number of students flip a given coin, it will end up in its original state – and that is heads up. If an odd number of flips take place, then the coin will end up in the tails up position. Let's have a look at how that works with the first ten coins:

Coin No. 1 is flipped by Student No. 1 and no others. One is an odd number, so Coin No. 1 will end up as tails up.

Coin No. 2 is flipped first by Student No. 1 and then flipped a second time by Student No. 2 and no others. That is a total of 2 flips. 2 is even, so Coin No. 2 will end up as heads up.

Coin No. 3 is flipped two times by Students No. 1 and 3. An even number of flips means final status is heads up.

Coin No. 4 flipped by Students No. 1, 2 and 4. 3 flips. Odd number. Final status: Tails up.

Coin No. 5 flipped by 2 students. 1 and 5. Even. Heads up.

Coin No. 6 flipped by 4 students. 1, 2, 3 and 6. Even. Heads up.

Coin No. 7 flipped by 2 students. 1 and 7. Even. Heads up.

Coin No. 8 flipped by 4 students. 1, 2, 4 and 8. Even. Heads up.

Coin No. 9 flipped by 3 students. 1, 3 and 9. Odd. Tails up.

Coin No. 10 flipped by 4 students. 1, 2, 5 and 10. Even. Heads up.

Do you detect a pattern? The coins that ended tails up were Nos. 1, 4 and 9. These are all "perfect square" numbers (1 squared = 1, 2 squared = 4, 3 squared = 9). Why is this so?

To understand this, we must look at the factors for each number. The factors are the integers that may be multiplied together to produce a given number.

How many factors are there for the number one? One. $1 \times 1 = 1$. An odd number of factors.

How many factors are there for the number two? Two. $1 \times 2 = 2$ and $2 \times 1 = 2$. An even number of factors.

How many factors are there for the number three? Two. $1 \times 3 = 3$ and $3 \times 1 = 3$. An even number.

For the number 4? Three. $1 \times 4 = 4$, $2 \times 2 = 4$, $4 \times 1 = 4$. An odd number.

For the number 5? Two. $1 \times 5 = 5$, $5 \times 1 = 5$. Even.

Number 6? Four. $1 \times 6 = 6$, $2 \times 3 = 6$, $3 \times 2 = 6$, $6 \times 1 = 6$. Even.

Number 7? Two. $1 \times 7 = 7$, $7 \times 1 = 7$. Even.

Number 8? Four. 1×8, 2×4, 4×2, 8×1. Even.

Number 9? Three. $1 \times 9 = 9$, $3 \times 3 = 9$, $9 \times 1 = 9$. Odd.

Number 10? Four. $1 \times 10 = 10$, $2 \times 5 = 10$, $5 \times 2 = 10$, $10 \times 1 = 10$. Even.

As shown, only numbers that are perfect squares have an odd number of factors. And if a coin has an odd number of flips, that means that the final status will be tails up. So now it becomes a simple matter to count up the perfect squares between 1 and 100 inclusive. There are ten, and here they are:

1, 4, 9, 16, 25, 36, 49, 64, 81 and 100.

The correct answers: 10 coins will end up as tails up and 90 coins will end up as heads up.

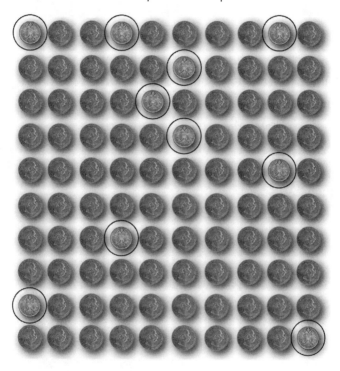

GENDER MIND BENDER

If one of Moishe's two kids is a girl, the odds that the other one is also girl are NOT 50%.

Prior to informing us that one of his kids is, in fact, a girl, there were four possibilities:

Boy-Boy, Boy-Girl, Girl-Boy, and Girl-Girl.

But when we find out that Moishe has at least one girl, the first one is ruled out, leaving three remaining possibilities.

Only one of the three contains two girls.

So the correct probability of both kids being girls, after we learn that one of them is a girl, is one out of three or 33.33%.

THE HAY AND THE HORSE

The other end of the rope wasn't tied to anything.

THE CAKE AND THE KINDER

"Tell this to your three children," advised the rabbi:

We'll draw names out of a hat to see who goes first, second, and third. Kid No. 1 cuts the cake into two pieces and Kid No. 2 picks either piece, leaving the remaining piece for Kid No. 1.

Now both Kid No. 1 and Kid No. 2 cut their pieces into three smaller pieces.

Kid No. 3 then takes one piece from No. 1 and one piece from No. 2.

No. 1 and No. 2 then put their remaining pieces all back together on the plate forming one big piece. This piece is then divided between No. 1 and No. 2 using the "one-picks-and-the-other chooses" method. Done.

What about collusion?

Since independent decisions are required of all three kids, there is no way to beat the system by making a secret deal in advance.

Let's suppose that No. 1 and No. 2 try to make a secret deal. "We'll fix it so No. 3 is short-changed and gets less than a third. Then we'll put our two pieces together and split the whole thing evenly between us." Sounds good, but it will not succeed. Here's why:

Let's say Kid No. 1 makes the first cut and divides the cake into uneven ⅓ and ⅔-sized pieces. Kid No. 2 naturally picks the larger, ⅔-sized piece.

Now, both Kid No. 1 and Kid No. 2 divide their respective pieces evenly into three. So Kid No. 2 winds up with three even pieces, each one equal to $\frac{2}{9}$ of the original cake ($\frac{1}{3} \times \frac{2}{3}$) or 22.22%.

Kid No. 1 winds up with three pieces, each equal to $\frac{1}{9}$ of the original cake ($\frac{1}{3} \times \frac{1}{3}$) or 11.11%.

So, Kid No. 3 picks one of No. 1's pieces and one of No. 2's pieces and winds up with two pieces that total $\frac{1}{3}$ of the original cake ($\frac{2}{9}$ plus $\frac{1}{9} = \frac{3}{9}$ or $\frac{1}{3}$ or 11.11% plus 22.22% equals 33.33%). No. 1 is left with two pieces of 11.11% each, or 22.22%. No. 2 is left with two pieces of 22.22% each or 44.44%. No. 1's plus No. 2's pieces are now combined to form one big piece equaling 66.67% of the original.

They flip a coin, and No. 2 is selected to cut while No. 1 selected to choose. No. 2 divides the one big piece perfectly in half, giving 33.33% to No. 1 and leaving 33.33% for himself.

All three kids wind up with one third of the cake with no chance of any collusion.

RUNNING IN THE RAIN

The yard was a graveyard. The four men were pall bearers. The fifth man was inside the coffin.

GETTING OFF THE ISLAND

The fellow observed the guard going in and out of the guardhouse. As soon as he saw the guard go in, the fellow walked across the bridge for four minutes. At that point, he turned around. When he came out of the guardhouse, the guard observed the man walking towards the island. When the fellow arrived to the island side of the bridge, the guard demanded 1,000 shekels. When the fellow explained that he didn't have the money, the guard ordered him to go back to the mainland.

THE BUSY BULBUL BIRD

The first thing the kids had to do was to figure out where the trains were when they met. Since the train from Minsk was moving twice as fast as the train from Pinsk, it covered twice as much ground in the same amount of time.

Therefore, the two trains met at a spot that was twice as far from Minsk as from Pinsk. That point can only be located at a spot 100 km from Pinsk and 200 km from Minsk.

Next question: How long have the two trains each been traveling by the time they met?

If the train from Minsk has covered 200 km traveling at a speed of 100 kph, that means it had been traveling for two hours by the time it reached the meeting point.

Likewise, if the train from Pinsk has covered 100 km traveling at a speed of 50 kph, then it also had been traveling for two hours by the time it reached the meeting point.

The bulbul bird had been flying nonstop for the same amount of time as the trains have been traveling. That is, two hours at a speed of 150 kph. That means it had flown a distance of 300 km by the times the two trains met.

DOMINOS AND CHESS

There are 32 black and 32 white alternating squares on a chessboard. When a domino is placed on the board it covers two adjacent squares. By necessity, one of the squares must be white and the other black. Therefore, if one domino is placed on the board, it will leave a matching number of black squares and white squares (31) uncovered. No matter how many dominos are placed on the board, the remaining uncovered squares will always be half white and half black.

A look at a chessboard reveals that the squares at opposite corners of the board are always the same color. Therefore it is impossible to leave either two white or two black squares uncovered after all 31 dominos have been placed on the board.

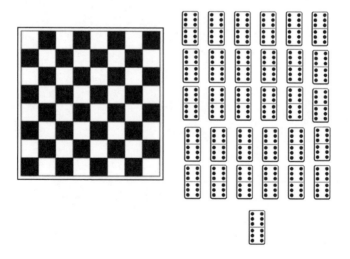

FROM THE BALCONY

Mr. Nussbaum was in seat number 87. Mrs. Nussbaum was looking at the numbers upside-down.

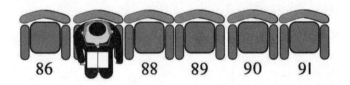

86   88   89   90   91

PITA PARTY PUZZLE

Nadav placed one pita on top of the other and sliced them both as shown:

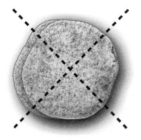

EQUATION OCCASION

$$5 \; 4 \; 3 + 70 = 613$$

About the Author

Peter Weisz has been collecting and authoring puzzles for years. He is an educator, author and publisher of personal history books. He lives in West Palm Beach, Florida.

Website: www.peterweisz.com
Email: peter@peterweisz.com